I'M THE BIGGEST!
IN THE OCEANS

LAURA K. MURRAY

CREATIVE EDUCATION   CREATIVE PAPERBACKS

CONT

4 Let's Explore the Oceans!

7 Ocean Depths

11 Staying Shallow for Sunlight

14 Animals, Big and Small

18 Full of Life

20
In the Oceans

22
Word Review

23
Read More & Websites

24
Index

LET'S EXPLORE THE OCEANS!

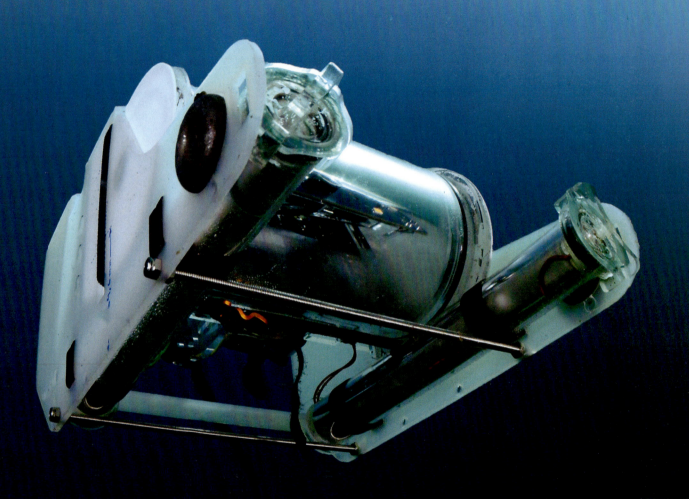

Water stretches out as far as you can see. Your drone camera captures a giant shadow swimming below the waves. It is a massive blue whale!

Ocean Depths

The ocean gets colder and darker as it gets deeper. The deepest place on Earth is in the Pacific Ocean. It is known as Challenger Deep. It is approximately 36,200 feet (11,034 m) deep.

Mount Everest
29,029 ft (8,848 m)

sea level

Challenger Deep
36,200 ft (11,034 m)

Tamu Massif (below) is an underwater **shield volcano**. It is located in the Pacific Ocean. Tamu Massif is the biggest volcano on Earth. It covers more than 100,000 square miles (258,999 sq km).

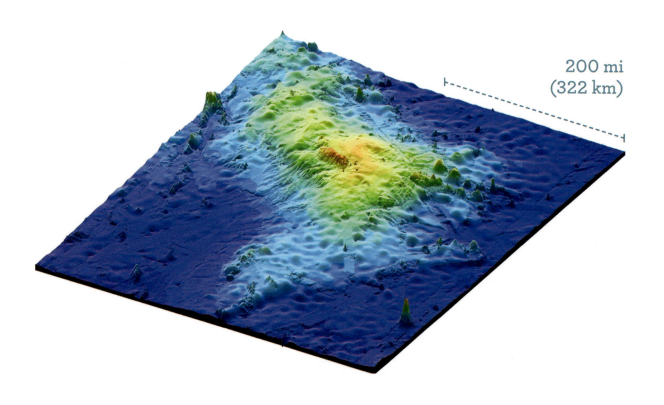

200 mi
(322 km)

shield volcano - a broad, domed volcano (a mountain with an opening at the top where lava and gases burst out)

algae - plant-like organisms that do not have stems, roots, or leaves

Staying Shallow for Sunlight

Ocean plants and **algae** are important food sources. They also provide much of the planet's oxygen. Plants and algae need sunlight to grow. Sunlight can reach 650 feet (198 m) into the ocean. Little grows deeper than this.

Seaweed is a type of large algae. Giant kelp is a seaweed that grows up to 175 feet (53.3 m) long. Other algae, such as phytoplankton, are so small they are **microscopic**.

microscopic - able to be seen only through a microscope

Animals, Big and Small

The blue whale is the biggest animal in the world! It grows up to 105 feet (32 m) long. It weighs 200 tons (181 t). The blue whale's calls are louder than a jet engine.

Japanese spider crabs are some of the biggest **arthropods**. Their legs span 18 feet (5.5 m). These animals live on the ocean floor at about 1,000 feet (305 m) deep. Fangtooth fish can live thousands of feet deeper. They are only six inches (15.2 cm) long.

fangtooth fish
actual size

arthropods - animals including insects, crustaceans (such as crabs, lobsters, and shrimp), or spiders

Full of Life

From algae to blue whales, the ocean is full of life. What other amazing things can you discover about this mysterious place?

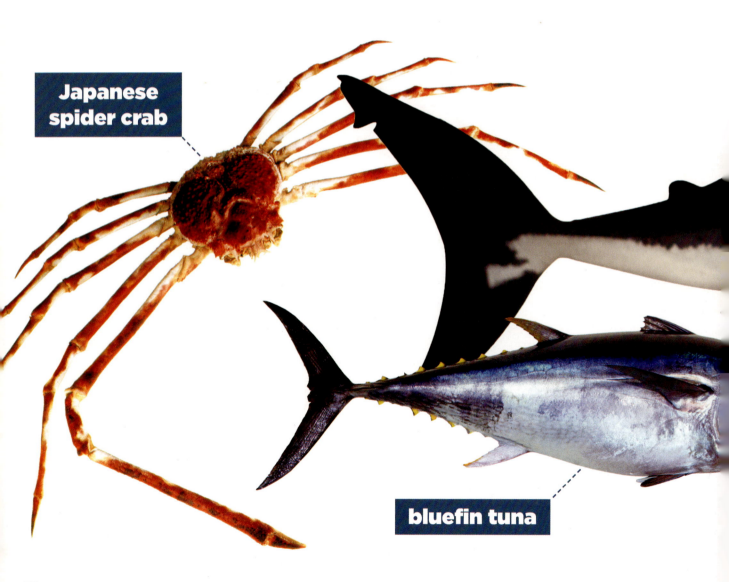

IN THE OCEANS

Oceans as percentages of the global ocean, smallest to largest:

5
Arctic Ocean
4.3%

4
Southern Ocean
6.1%

3
Indian Ocean
19.5%

2
Atlantic Ocean
23.5%

1
Pacific Ocean
46.6%

Word Review

Do you remember what these words mean? Look at the pictures for clues, and go back to the page where the words were defined, if you need help.

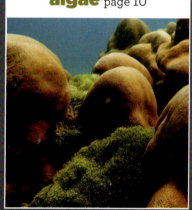
algae page 10

arthropods page 17

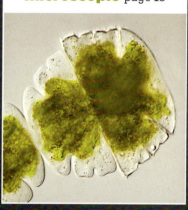
microscopic page 13

shield volcano page 8

Read More

Oachs, Emily Rose. *Pacific Ocean*.
Minneapolis: Bellwether Media, 2016.

Riggs, Kate. *Oceans*.
Mankato, Minn.: Creative Education, 2010.

Websites

NASA Climate Kids: Ocean

https://climatekids.nasa.gov/menu/ocean/

Learn more about ocean weather, plants, and animals.

National Geographic Kids: Ocean Portal

http://kids.nationalgeographic.com/explore/ocean-portal/

Find articles, games, and videos about ocean life.

Note: Every effort has been made to ensure that the websites listed above are suitable for children, that they have educational value, and that they contain no inappropriate material. However, because of the nature of the Internet, it is impossible to guarantee that these sites will remain active indefinitely or that their contents will not be altered.

Index

algae   11, 13, 18
    giant kelp   13
    phytoplankton   13
blue whales   5, 14, 18
Challenger Deep   7
depths   7, 11, 17
fangtooth fish   17
Japanese spider crabs   17
Pacific Ocean   8, 21
plants   11
Tamu Massif   8

PUBLISHED BY CREATIVE EDUCATION AND CREATIVE PAPERBACKS

P.O. Box 227, Mankato, Minnesota 56002
Creative Education and Creative Paperbacks are imprints of The Creative Company
www.thecreativecompany.us

LIBRARY OF CONGRESS CATALOGING-IN-PUBLICATION DATA

Names: Murray, Laura K., author.
Title: In the oceans / Laura K. Murray.
Series: I'm the biggest.
Summary: From shortest to longest and biggest to smallest, this ecosystem investigation uses varying degrees of comparison to take a closer look at the relationships of ocean flora, fauna, and landforms.

Identifiers: ISBN 978-1-64026-062-7 (hardcover)
ISBN 978-1-62832-650-5 (pbk)
ISBN 978-1-64000-178-7 (eBook)
This title has been submitted for CIP processing under LCCN 2018938956.

CCSS: RI.1.1, 2, 4, 5, 6, 7; RI.2.1, 2, 5, 6, 7; RI.3.1, 2, 5, 7; RF.1.1, 3, 4; RF.2.3, 4

COPYRIGHT © 2019 CREATIVE EDUCATION, CREATIVE PAPERBACKS

International copyright reserved in all countries. No part of this book may be reproduced in any form without written permission from the publisher.

DESIGN AND PRODUCTION

by Joe Kahnke; art direction by Rita Marshall
Printed in the United States of America

PHOTOGRAPHS by Alamy (The Natural History Museum, Leonid Serebrennikov), Corbis (Mike Parry/Minden Pictures), Creative Commons Wikimedia (IODP), Dreamstime (Isabellebonaire, Steven Melanson), FreeVectorMaps.com, Getty Images (ANATOLI MYSHLYAEV/Moment, Humberto Ramirez/Moment, Michael Zeigler/E+), iStockphoto (LUNAMARINA, MarcelloLand, mihtiander, Myroslava, petesphotography, sara_winter, Soft_Light, SteveAllenPhoto), Minden Pictures (Norbert Wu, Tony Wu/NPL), Shutterstock (Heitor Barbosa, blojfo, Allen Haggerty, Hayk_Shalunts, igorstevanovic, Eric Isselee, Haripat Jantawalee, KenshiDesign, Pataporn Kuanui, Lebendkulturen.de, Jolanta Wojcicka)

FIRST EDITION HC 9 8 7 6 5 4 3 2 1
FIRST EDITION PBK 9 8 7 6 5 4 3 2 1